Y0-BFA-380

HOW TO SET UP YOUR
DRUMSET
the most complete reference guide available

Cover photo courtesy of Yamaha Corporation of America

Photos on pp. 4, 21, 22, 23, 24, 25, 26, 27, pedaling photos on pp. 11 & 12, photo on bottom of p. 15, photo at middle of p. 16, and hi-hat photos on pp. 18 & 19 by Jeff Leland.

Photos at top of p. 8 and top of p. 9 by Karen Miller.

Photos on pp. 29 & 30 © Alfred Publishing Co., Inc.

All other interior photos courtesy of Yamaha Corporation of America.

Copyright © MMII by Alfred Publishing Co., Inc.
All rights reserved.   Printed in USA.
ISBN 0-7390-2455-8

Dave Black

CONTENTS

PREFACE

Since the inception of the drumset at the turn of the twentieth century, the primary role of the drumset player has been that of an accompanist, functioning not only as the metronome or time keeper, but also as the creator of basic beats and patterns from which playing is based within various styles.

Over the years, the components of the "standard" drumset have changed as musical styles and tastes have evolved. For example, during the 1940s and 1950s, the standard drumset consisted of four drums (snare, bass, a mounted tom and floor tom), a ride cymbal, crash cymbal, pair of hi-hat cymbals, and perhaps some accessory instruments such as a cowbell and woodblock. With the evolution of rock 'n' roll, pop, etc., the cowbell and woodblock were replaced by an additional tom, making the standard drumset a five-piece setup rather than a four-piece setup. During the 1960s and 1970s, the size of the drumset increased considerably with the addition of multiple toms, a second bass drum, specialty cymbals (sizzle, Chinese, splash, etc.), and even more accessory instruments (wind chimes, roto-toms, electronic trigger pads, etc.).

Today, a "standard" drumset is a four- or five-piece setup containing the four basic elements: drums, cymbals, hardware (stands, mounting devices and pedals) and throne (or stool). A standard five-piece set includes a snare drum, bass drum (with a bass drum pedal), two mounted tom-toms (with mounting hardware), a floor tom-tom, cymbals (with stands), a hi-hat stand and a drum throne. As mentioned above, additional drums, including an additional bass drum, cymbals and accessory instruments, may be added to the basic setup.

Special thanks to:
Dave Tull, Rod Harbour, Dave White, Kate Westin, Kim Kasabian, Steve Harder, Link Harnsberger, Bruce Goldes, Yamaha Corp. of America and Guitar Center.

THE OVERALL SETUP

The drums and cymbals should be centralized around the player in such a way as to minimize reaching, stretching and twisting. The drums should be set up to accommodate the player—not the reverse.

Comfortable positioning of the drumset and a relaxed approach will help to facilitate smooth motion. The type of motion employed in playing will be reflected in the quality of sound. Relaxed motions will produce smooth, controlled sounds, while stiff motions will produce tight, constrained sounds. It is important that you strive for a relaxed approach.

THE DRUM AND ITS PARTS

Many parts are common to all drums of a drumset. The snare drum is used here as a model for pointing out the various features. Parts specific to individual drums are addressed in the appropriate sections.

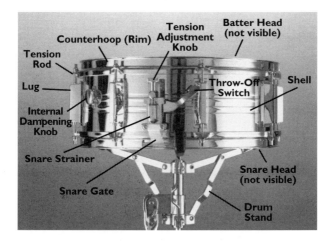

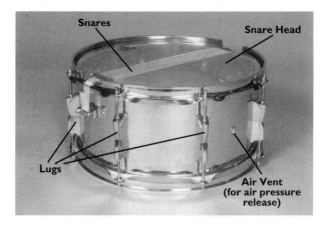

1. The top head of the snare drum is referred to as the _batter head_, and is available with either a smooth finish or rough, sand-like coating. The bottom head is called the _snare head_. As a general rule, the bottom head should be thinner and slightly tighter than the batter head. In most cases, the batter head will determine the timbre of the drum, but this, of course, will depend on the thickness, resonance and condition of the head.

2. The *flesh hoop* (originally a wooden piece around which damp calfskin was tucked) is a ring, usually metal, to which the head is attached by means of glue or pressure.

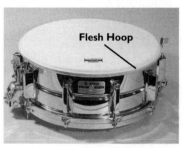

3. Drumheads are held in place by *counter-hoops*, also referred to as *rims*. They are made of either metal or wood and sit on top of the flesh hoop, holding the head onto the rim with the help of *tension rods*.

4. The *shell* is the frame that supports all the other components of the drum. It may be constructed of wood, sometimes with a lacquer or pearl finish, or made of metal or fiberglass.

5. The *bearing edge* is the point on the snare drum where the head meets the rim. Usually cut at a 45-degree angle, this edge must evenly touch the drumhead to insure its proper seating on the shell.

6. *Lugs* are attached to the side of the drum shell and serve as receptacles for the tension rods.

7. *Tension rods* hold the counterhoop in place and are used to adjust the tension of the drumhead. The number of rods and lugs attached to the snare drum depends upon the size of the drum, but the usual number is 8 to10 for most drums.

8. The *air vent* is a hole in the side of the drum shell that allows air to escape when the batter head is struck.

9. The *snare strainer*, also called the *snare release*, allows the snares to be engaged or disengaged from the snare head by means of a throw-off switch.

10. The *tension adjustment knob* is located on top of the throw-off switch. Turning it clockwise or counter-clockwise allows you to adjust the tension or pressure of the snares as they lie across the bottom head.

11. _Snares_ are wire, gut or plastic strands that stretch across the outside surface of the bottom head.

    a. Gut snares are made of catgut. They produce a dark, crisp and articulate sound, but are lacking in the ability to respond at softer dynamic levels. Like calfskin heads, they can be affected by weather and are commonly used in the marching field.

    b. Wire snares are made of coiled, spring-like strands. They have a bright sound and respond well at lower dynamic levels. As a result, they are the preferred choice of concert percussionists and drumset players.

    c. Plastic (nylon) snares are brighter than gut snares and are not affected by weather. They are articulate, and effective for marching use.

12. The _tone control_ or _internal dampening knob_ is mounted on the outside of the shell and attached to an internal muffler. When the knob is turned clockwise, the muffler presses against the batter head to absorb some of the vibrations and eliminate the after-ring.

The Snare Drum

1. A standard snare drum is 14 inches in diameter. (Some drummers may also use a 13-inch piccolo snare drum.)

Piccolo Snare Drum

2. The components of the snare drum are the shell (made of either wood, metal or fiberglass), two counterhoops (rims), lugs and tension rods (the number of which depends on the size of the drum), a _snare head_ and a _batter head_, a _snare strainer_ (which includes a throw-off switch/snare adjustment screw), a muffler (operated by an internal dampening knob) and the snares (made of either wire, nylon or gut). See photo on page 5.

3. The drum is placed on top of a stand, referred to as the "*cradle*." Once securely in the cradle, a screw at the bottom of the cradle allows the stand to be tightened around the circumference of the drum.

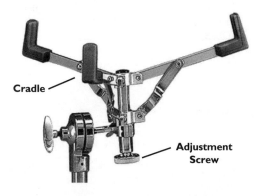

The height of the stand may be adjusted to fit the player's needs.

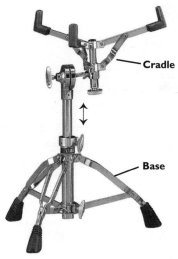

4. The drum should be placed to the right of the hi-hat and rotated so that the throw-off switch is easily accessible.

5. Whether played with matched or traditional grip, the snare drum should be positioned and angled so that the proper alignment of the forearms and hands is not affected.

    a. With matched grip, the snare drum is usually flat or slanted slightly downward and toward the player.

b. With traditional grip, the snare drum is usually tilted slightly downward and (if right-handed) to the right.

The Bass Drum

1. The bass drum, also referred to as the *kick drum*, is usually between 18 to 26 inches in diameter, 22 inches being the most common. It may have one or two heads. A second bass drum may be added to the basic five-piece setup.

2. The components of the bass drum are a shell (made of either wood or fiberglass), two counterhoops (rims), lugs and tension rods (the number of which depends on the size of the drum), a tom-tom mount (for either one or two tom-toms), one or two heads, and two spurs (one attached to each side) to keep the drum from tilting side to side or sliding forward (see photo above).

3. The use of a rug or mat is strongly recommended, as it will not only protect floors and the bottom of the drum, but will help keep the drum from sliding forward as it is being played.

The Bass Drum Pedal and
Pedal Tension Adjustment

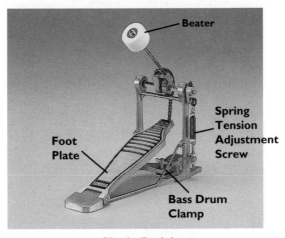

Single Pedal

1. The bass drum is played with a single or double bass drum pedal, clamped to the rim of the bass drum and operated by the foot. In addition to the foot plate, it consists of a beater and a spring tension adjustment screw.

2. Varieties of beater types are available for the bass drum pedal. The following are brief descriptions of the main beater types.

   • Medium Felt Beater: This is a good, general-purpose beater capable of producing a medium punch or fatter attack. It is more dense than the large felt beater, and is good for medium-volume music.

   • Large Felt Beater: This beater is larger than a medium felt beater, and less dense. It is primarily used to produce a tone that is deeper in timbre, but not usually one with a loud punch or attack.

   • Rubber Beater: Because this beater is more dense than one made of felt, it will deliver a stronger punch. It will not, however, produce as much punch or attack as one made of plastic or wood.

   • Wood/Plastic Beater: Beaters made of plastic or wood are very dense and heavy. They are capable of producing very powerful and sharp attacks, and are especially good for rock and Latin applications.

   • Two-Way Beater: A good combination of

felt on one side and hard plastic on the other, this beater can produce both tones of felt and wood. Because the plastic side is similar to wood, it is capable of producing a very powerful and sharp attack. This beater is used in a variety of musical styles because of its versatility.

3. After the beater strikes the drumhead, the spring returns the beater to its original position unless the return stroke has been restricted by pressing the beater against the head.

4. Adjust the pedal's spring tension to offer firm resistance to the action of the foot pedal. The tighter the tension, the faster the rebound of the pedal.

5. Two fundamental techniques for playing the bass drum are *heel up* and *heel down*.

    • Heel Down: In this technique, the entire foot contacts the pedal. The player rocks the foot with an ankle motion, causing the beater to strike the head. The foot then returns immediately to the "up" position, without leaving the pedal as shown in photos 1a and 1b.

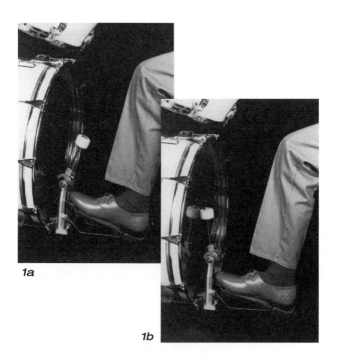

1a

1b

- Heel Up: In this technique (often used for louder, more articulate strokes), the heel is raised one to two inches off the pedal surface, while the ball of the foot operates the pedal. The foot returns immediately to the "up" position as shown in photos 2a and 2b. For greater volume, the leg may be used in conjunction with the ankle.

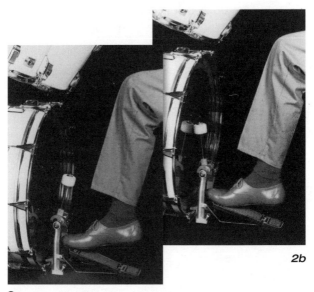

2b

2a

6. Rebound techniques, as applied to the snare drum, apply to the bass drum as well.

The Mounted (Rack) Tom-Toms

Tom-Tom Mount

Counterhoop (Rim)

Tension Rod

Shell

Lug

Drumhead

Tom-Tom Mount (attached to Bass Drum)

1. One or more mounted toms may be used, ranging in size from 6 to18 inches in diameter, 12 or 13 inches being the most common.

2. "Power" drum sizes are also available, which extend the depth of the shell to create a lower pitch and darker sound than that of the traditional tom-tom. These particular drums may increase the overall volume and

height of the drumset because of the extended length of the tom-toms mounted on the bass drum.

3. The components of the tom-tom are a shell (made of either wood or fiberglass), two counterhoops (rims), lugs and tension rods (the number of which depends on the size of the drum), one or two heads, and a mount (attached to the side of the drum) to secure it to the top of the bass drum.

4. The tom-toms should be tuned before attaching them to the bass drum, as it will become more difficult to do once they've been put in place (see *How to Tune Your Drums,* #20426, for a complete explanation.)

5. Attach the tom-toms to the mount on top of the bass drum. Tilt the drums slightly toward you in such a way that you clear the rims while striking the heads comfortably with the side of the stick tip (see photo below). Avoiding a severe drumstick angle will not only produce the best tone, but will also reduce the likelihood of damaging the drumhead. If using more than one mounted tom, large gaps in height between the batter heads of the drums should be avoided, as well as large distances between each drum.

The Floor Tom-Tom

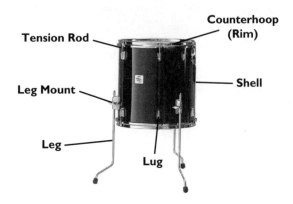

1. The largest of the tom-toms, the floor tom usually ranges in size from 14 to 16 inches in diameter, 16 inches being the most common. It may have one or two heads.

2. The components of the floor tom-tom are a shell (made of either wood or fiberglass), two counterhoops (rims), lugs and tension rods (the number of which depends on the size of the drum), and three legs (or a stand with mount) that can be adjusted to fit your needs.

3. Place the floor tom to the right of the snare drum at approximately the same height. It may be angled slightly toward you or toward the snare drum.

When more than one floor tom-tom is used, large gaps in height between the batter heads of the drums should be avoided, as well as large distances between each drum.

The Throne (Stool)

The position and height of the drum throne is critical to proper balance, and directly affects the flexibility and performance of the feet.

Because each person is built differently, throne adjustments are of a personal nature (as are most drumset positions). It is crucial, however, to find a height and distance that will allow total relaxation, specifically of the hips, legs, ankles and upper body. If you experience pain in your lower back, additional adjustments will need to be made.

Adjust the throne height so the hip is slightly above the knee when sitting. Draw an imaginary straight line vertically from the front of your knee to the back of your foot. In this position, the ligaments, tendons and muscles are flexible and free to move naturally whether you play heel up or heel down. (Stretching exercises will help achieve maximum flexibility.) From this position, make slight height and distance adjustments to suit your own personal needs. Remember that if you sit too close or far away from the drumset, your limbs may move unnaturally and cause undo stress on your joints, ligaments and muscles. This, in turn, will minimize flexibility when playing. Remember—always set the drums up to *you*!

ARRANGING DRUMSET CYMBALS

The standard cymbal setup will include a ride cymbal, one or two crash cymbals and a pair of hi-hat cymbals (see photo below). Most drummers will have at least two crash cymbals before adding additional specialty cymbals to their setup.

If you are using several cymbals, it is wise to arrange them around yourself in such a way as to minimize reaching, stretching and twisting. The exact placement, of course, will depend on your physical size and technical ability. Proper cymbal positioning will help to assure optimum sound quality and volume while minimizing the possibility of damage to the cymbal.

The Hi-Hat

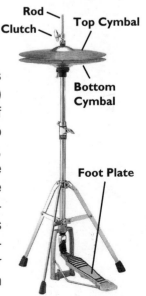

1. The hi-hat (sometimes called the *sock cymbal*) consists of a pair of cymbals, usually 14 to 15 inches in diameter, mounted "facing" one above the other. The most popular combination of hi-hat cymbals is a medium-thin top cymbal and a medium or medium-heavy bottom cymbal.

2. The cymbals are placed on a special stand that includes an adjustable tension spring in its shaft (right), and a foot pedal attached to a rod. When the pedal is pressed, the top cymbal is lowered onto the bottom one.

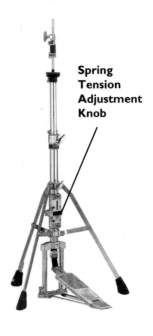

Spring Tension Adjustment Knob

3. The bottom cymbal rests on top of a felt-covered platform. The top cymbal is held by felt pads and a special mounting bracket called a *clutch*. The clutch is attached to a rod that moves up and down with the pedal.

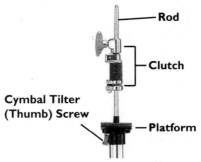

Rod

Clutch

Cymbal Tilter (Thumb) Screw

Platform

When at rest, the space between the two cymbals should be approximately 1 to 2 inches.

I to 2 inches

4. The hi-hat should be placed to the left of (and slightly higher than) the snare drum, and operated (by a right-handed player) with the left foot.

5. When the foot pedal is pressed, the cymbals are brought together to produce a crisp, "chick" sound. (Note: If the cymbals are perfectly parallel to one another, no sound will result. Use the thumb screw located beneath the bottom cymbal to tilt it slightly, thereby producing the distinctive "chick" sound.)

6. The hi-hat spring's tension should be adjusted to offer firm resistance to the foot pedal's action. The tighter the tension, the faster the rebound of the pedal.

7. Two fundamental techniques for playing the hi-hat are *heel-toe (rocking)* and *toe*.

   • The *heel-toe* or *rocking* technique is often used when playing repetitive strokes on beats 2 and 4. As the ball of the foot presses the pedal down on beats 2 and 4, the heel rises off the pedal; on beats 1 and 3, the ball of the foot rises as the heel goes back down.

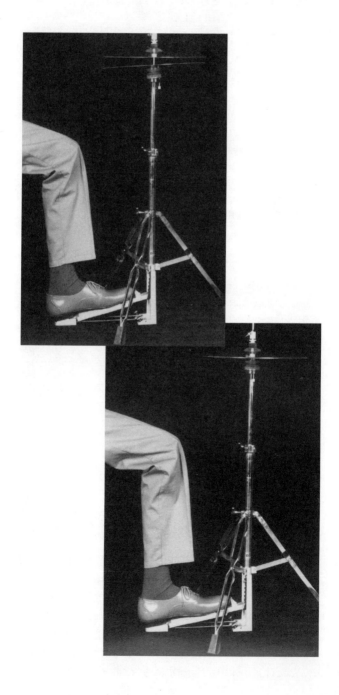

- The *toe* technique is particularly useful for executing rapid or unusual rhythms. When using this technique, the leg is raised to lift the heel from the pedal while the ball of the foot is bounced up and down to activate the hi-hat. Keep your leg relaxed and ankle flexible so the foot feels like it is being bounced rather than lifted up by the leg.

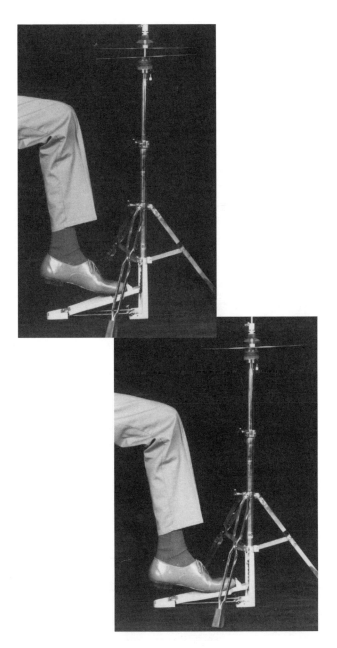

Playing on the Hi-Hat

1. As an alternative to the ride cymbal, the hi-hat can be played with a drumstick (using the tip or shoulder) to strike the top hi-hat cymbal, creating an articulate, ostinato effect. This is particularly effective in rock and Latin styles.

2. The hi-hat may also be played while the cymbals are open, partially closed (cymbals lightly touching to provide a looser, "swishing" sound) or completely closed. A plus (+) sign represents a closed hi-hat; an open hi-hat is designated by a letter o (o). Accented notes may be produced by striking the edge of the hi-hat with the shoulder of the stick. Non-accented notes are produced by striking the top of the hi-hat (not the bell) with the tip of the stick.

Additional Hi-Hat Cymbal Types

Aside from the basic hi-hat setup described above, there are a variety of specialized hi-hat cymbals available that can produce a wide range of sounds. Some of these additional cymbal types include flat, sizzle and rippled-edge hi-hats.

Flat

Sizzle

Rippled Edge

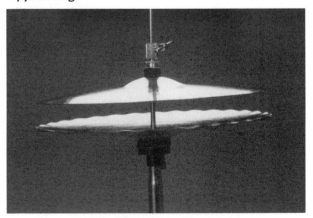

The Ride Cymbal

1. The function of the ride cymbal is to maintain an ostinato beat or pattern. Because greater volume and projection is required, ride cymbals are generally thicker and larger than other cymbal types.

2. A ride cymbal is usually 18 to 22 inches in diameter, and medium to medium-heavy in weight. It should be positioned in such a way as to allow the stick to strike 2 to 4 inches in from the edge. You should not have to extend your upper arm from its natural hanging position in order to reach the playing areas of the cymbal.

3. The ride cymbal should be mounted on a cymbal stand, supported by a metal washer covered with felt (right). The threaded tube should be sheathed in a piece of rubber or nylon tubing. A  felt pad should be placed on top of the cymbal so that the wing nut does not make contact with the cymbal (this would not only restrict the cymbal's sound, but may also cause the cymbal to crack as it vibrates widely on its axis).

4. Boom stands are also available and may be used for larger, heavier cymbals, offering greater flexibility when positioning them.

Playing the Ride Cymbal

1. The three main areas of the cymbal are the *edge*, *profile* or *bow* and *bell*.

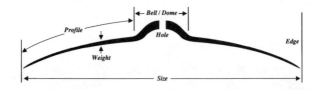

2. The ride cymbal may be struck in a variety of places to obtain different sounds. When it is struck on the bell, it will produce a high-pitched "ping" sound, effective for Latin-American rhythms or "funk" (see photos 1a and 1b).

1a.

1b.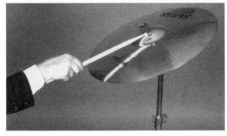

3. When struck near the edge, a ride cymbal will produce a broad sound with prominent midrange overtones.

4. About 2 to 4 inches in from the edge is considered to be the best area for playing the ride-cymbal pattern (see photo below).

The exact sound, however, is a matter of personal taste and preference.

5. A variety of interesting effects can be created by using the tip, shoulder and butt end of the drumstick on the ride cymbal.

6. Excessive ringing of a ride cymbal may be eliminated by placing two small strips of tape on the cymbal's underside (perhaps also to each side of the cymbal

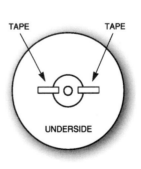

bell as shown in the following diagram). This is particularly effective when more definition and clarity is required, such as in a live room or in a recording studio. Obviously, tape may be removed when necessary without harming the cymbal.

The Crash Cymbal

1. The function of the crash cymbal is to punctuate, accent or reinforce a sudden "explosive" sound rather than to execute a particular rhythm. Because a quick attack and decay is required of this cymbal, it is generally thinner and smaller than a ride cymbal.

2. One or more crash cymbals may be used so that a cymbal can be matched with a particular sound. Crash cymbals usually range from 16 to 18 inches in diameter, and are from thin to medium in weight.

3. Crash cymbals are generally tilted slightly and positioned within normal reach so as to allow the drumstick's shaft to strike the cymbal's bow and/or edge at a 45-degree angle (see photo below).

Some drummers place their crash cymbals above normal playing height to maximize visual effect.

4. Extreme angling of a crash cymbal will restrict the cymbal's movement, diminish its response and put unnecessary pressure on the bell (cup) area. If a greater cymbal angle is desired, a cymbal tilter—often using a spring as a shock absorber—may be useful.

Playing the Crash Cymbal

It is suggested that you use a quick blow and follow-through when striking a crash cymbal. Never overplay a cymbal in order to produce more volume. If more power is needed, you should seek larger, heavier cymbals, which are not as likely to break during loud playing.

Choking the Crash Cymbal

Sometimes, it is desirable to shorten the after-ring of a crash cymbal. This is done by grabbing the cymbal's edge with the free hand as shown below.

Although this effect is more frequently applied to crash cymbals, it may be employed on cymbals of all types and in any setting, as needed.

Additional Cymbal Types

Aside from the basic cymbal setup described above, there is a variety of specialized cymbals available that can produce a wide range of sounds and sometimes visual effects. These cymbals come in a wide range of sizes, shapes, colors, weights and sound characteristics, and are frequently used by drummers to supplement their basic cymbal setup. Some of these additional cymbal types include sizzle, splash, Chinese, octagonal, flat-bell, minibell, megabell, flange-ride, grooveless, and cymbals with a colored finish.

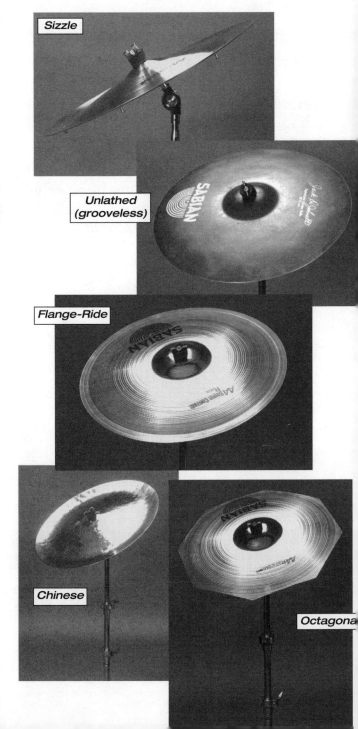

Sizzle

Unlathed (grooveless)

Flange-Ride

Chinese

Octagonal

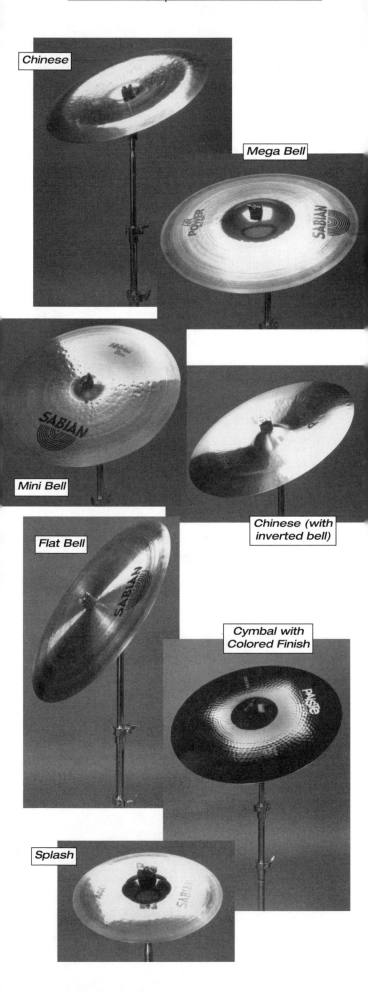

Chinese

Mega Bell

Mini Bell

Chinese (with inverted bell)

Flat Bell

Cymbal with Colored Finish

Splash

CHOOSING DRUMSTICKS AND MALLETS

1. Drumsticks come in a variety of sizes and shapes, designed for different sounds and/or applications. A stick with a small tip is articulate, whereas one with a larger, rounder tip produces a broad, full sound. The parts of the drumstick are the *butt end*, *shaft*, *shoulder*, *neck* and *bead* or *tip* (see diagram below).

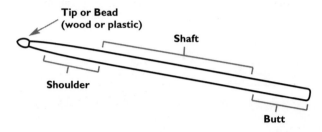

2. Snare drum sticks are most often made of wood (usually maple, oak or hickory). Plastic, fiberglass and metal have also been tried, but with limited success.

3. Sticks are available with either a wood or a nylon tip. Those with nylon tips are designed to produce a more articulated sound on the cymbals (especially useful for a repeating ostinato pattern). When used on a drum, however, they sound almost identical to a wood-tipped stick.

4. "A" model sticks (originally designed for jazz playing) are smaller than "B" model sticks (designed for heavier use in a concert band), which are smaller than "S" model sticks (intended for street or marching use), which are smaller than "DC" sticks (designed for drum-corp use).

5. For beginning snare drummers, a "2B" or "5B" model stick is recommended. For those playing in a jazz or concert band setting, a "5A" or "5B" drumstick is a good, standard stick to start with. For those playing in a rock or heavy metal band, a larger pair of sticks may be desired. Whatever your choice, you should always carry multiple pairs in the event they break or get lost.

6. When purchasing sticks, it is recommended that you check them carefully to make sure you're buying a matched pair. The following guidelines will help you make that determination.

a. Visually inspect each stick for obvious flaws.

b. Tap each stick on a hard surface and listen for an even match. Sticks that produce a high pitch are most likely made of dense wood, which is excellent for both sound and response.

c. Check to make sure the sticks are not warped by rolling each one on a hard, flat surface. Those that are warped should be discarded.

7. Because brushes produce the second most requested sound, every drummer should carry at least one pair. Brushes can be made of wire or nylon, be retractable or non-retractable, and have handles made of wood, plastic or metal. Like sticks, they come in a variety of sizes and weights.

8. A variety of mallets covered with yarn or felt is also recommended for use on the tom-toms (good for soft, muted sounds) or for suspended cymbal rolls.

9. A stick bag is recommended for the storage and transportation of your sticks, mallets and brushes. They come in a variety of sizes, styles, colors and materials, and can be attached to the side of the floor tom-tom for easy access while playing.

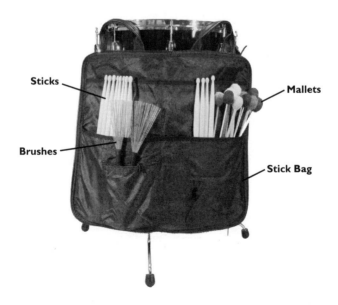

CARE AND MAINTENANCE
Cases/Storage

Proper care, storage and regular maintenance of your equipment will yield positive results for years to come.

1. When your drumset remains set up but is not being used, keep it covered with an old, but clean sheet or blanket to protect it from dust and dirt.

2. When your drumset is not in use for longer periods of time, place the drums in cases and store them where they are not subjected to either extreme cold or heat.

3. When transporting your drums and hardware, it is strongly recommended that you use any number of commercially available cases (either leather, canvas, nylon or fiber) designed specifically for the storage and transport of drums and hardware.

Drumheads

Drumheads should be kept free from dirt, and replaced when they become worn or broken. They may be cleaned with mild soap and water (though this is not common practice). Do not allow moisture to accumulate between the edge of the head and the counterhoop.

Drum Shells

Regular cleaning of your drums will help prolong their beauty and tone. Wood and pearl finishes may be cleaned with a damp cloth and mild soap; furniture polish may also be applied to wood finishes, if desired. Shells should be checked periodically for cracks.

Hardware

Tension rods should be lubricated with Vaseline or light grease. Those that are bent or stripped should be replaced. Moving parts, including the snare throw-off switch, bass drum pedal and hi-hat pedal, should be lubricated once or twice a year with light machine oil.

Metal shells and hoops may be cleaned with a damp cloth and/or metal polish. Broken snares, warped rims, and faulty strainers should be fixed or replaced immediately.

Storage and Shipment of Cymbals

1. Cymbals should not be stored where they will be subject to either extreme cold or heat, as a temporary loss of sound may occur until normal temperature has been restored.

2. When transporting cymbals, it is suggested that you use a leather, canvas or nylon-padded bag made specifically for cymbals. There are also fiber cases specifically designed for cymbal transport.

3. Bass drum and trap cases sometimes have special compartments for the specific purpose of carrying cymbals. If more than one cymbal is being carried or stored in a single bag or case, it is suggest that padding be used to separate the cymbals to prevent scratching.

Cleaning Cymbals

1. Fingerprints and dirt can be removed by using a solution of mild liquid dishwater detergent and warm water. Most cymbal manufactures market specially formulated cymbal-cleaning products as well. If further cleaning becomes necessary, there are a number of nonabrasive commercial cleansers available on the market.

2. Never use steel wool, wire brushes or any other abrasive cleanser. If a cymbal is exceptionally old and dirty, a stiff fiber

brush may be used. Never use an electric buffing device, as the heat generated will alter a cymbal's temper, making it vulnerable to cracking.

3. Cymbal felts and plastic sleeves on cymbal stands should be checked on a regular basis to make sure that the cymbal is not making contact with the stand.

Repairing Cymbal Cracks

1. Even with proper care and maintenance, cymbals can still develop cracks. If a crack occurs, it must be eliminated as soon as possible because eventually the smallest nick will develop into a large crack. Cracks up to about one-half inch can be ground out (see diagram below).

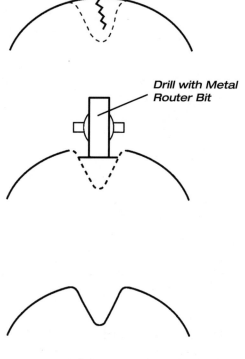

Drill with Metal Router Bit

2. Never attempt to braze or weld cymbals, as the heat will cause irreversible damage.

3. It is important to remember that these techniques have been proven successful in stopping cracks from spreading, but there is no guarantee they will work in all cases, or indefinitely.